LEARN TO DRAW

Disney
MICKEY
& FRIENDS

Illustrated by John Loter and the Disney Storybook Artists

Walter Foster Jr.

© 2018 Disney Enterprises, Inc.
Illustrated by John Loter and the Disney Storybook Artists.

Published by Walter Foster Jr., an imprint of The Quarto Group.
6 Orchard Road, Suite 100, Lake Forest, CA 92630, USA.
T (949) 380-7510 **F** (949) 380-7575 **www.QuartoKnows.com**

No license is herein granted for the use of any drawing of a Disney character for any commercial purpose, including, but not limited to, the placing of any such drawing on an article of merchandise or the reproduction, public display, or sale of any such drawing. Any use other than home use by the reader of any such drawing is prohibited.

ISBN: 978-1-63322-655-5

Printed in China
10 9 8 7 6 5 4 3 2 1

MIX
Paper from
responsible sources
FSC
www.fsc.org
FSC® C101537

TABLE OF CONTENTS

TOOLS & MATERIALS

You need to gather only a few simple art supplies before you begin. Start with a drawing pencil and an eraser. Make sure you also have a pencil sharpener and a ruler. To add color to your drawings, use markers, colored pencils, crayons, watercolors, or acrylic paint.
The choice is yours!

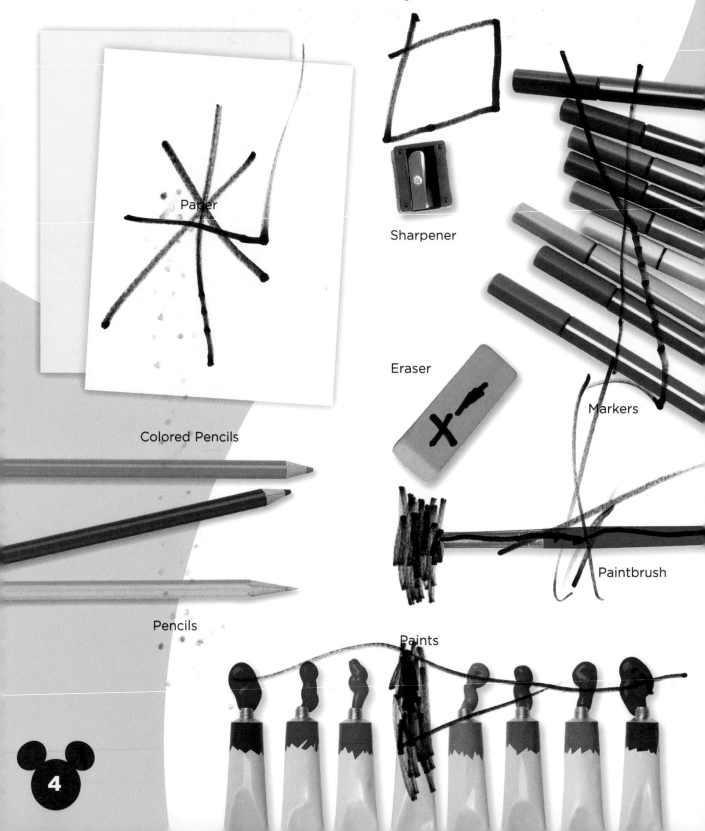

Paper

Sharpener

Eraser

Markers

Colored Pencils

Paintbrush

Pencils

Paints

TRACING BASICS

This book has five sheets of blank tracing paper, which you can use to trace the characters pictured on the pages after them.

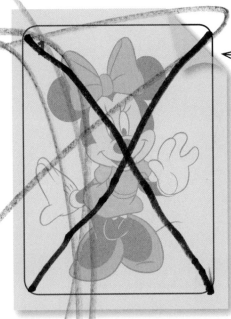

tracing paper

Make sure the tracing paper is placed over the character you want to draw. You should be able to see through the tracing paper.

With your pencil, draw everything you can see over the character you're tracing.

Pay close attention to all the little details.5

GRID METHOD

When using the grid method, focus on copying the lines and shapes in each square.
The lines of the grid will help you draw your lines and shapes in the correct places.

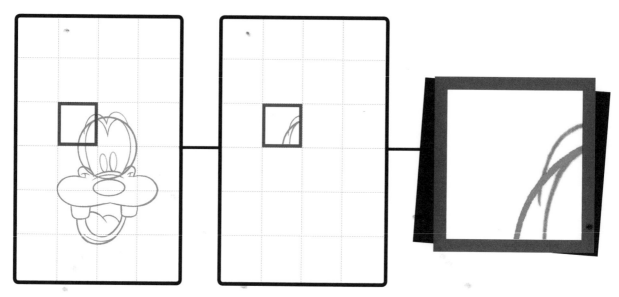

Copy everything you see in each square into the corresponding square on your blank
practice grid. Make sure you are copying the shapes and lines into the correct spot!

After you've completed all the lines in step one, move on to the next step and keep going!
Add color, and you're done!

BASIC SHAPES

When using the step-by-step drawing method, you will begin by drawing very basic shapes, such as lines and circles. At the end of each basic shapes project in this book, there is a blank page where you can practice drawing.

3

In each new step, add more defining lines.

2

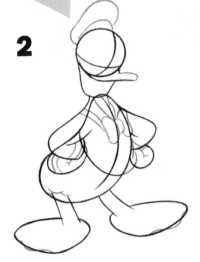

Pay attention to the new lines added in each step.

1

First draw the basic shapes, using light lines that will be easy to erase.

5

Add color to your drawing with colored pencils, markers, paints, or crayons!

4

Erase guidelines and add more detail.

MICKEY MOUSE

Mickey Mouse is kind and cheerful, brave, curious, and a great pal. He enjoys everyday pleasures, such as the company of his girlfriend Minnie, friends, or a walk outdoors with his faithful dog, Pluto. Mickey loves laughter and fun but is also prepared to meet any challenge that comes his way.

Use the tracing paper to draw Mickey.

Step 1

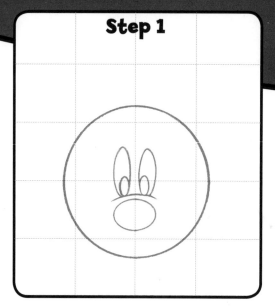

Step 2

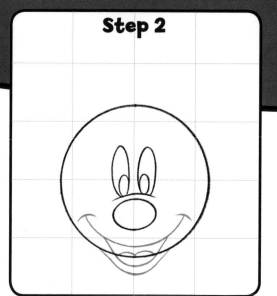

Step 3

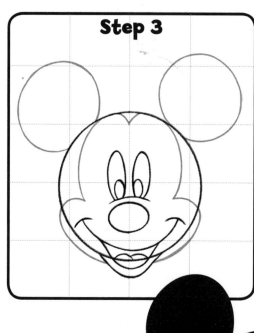

Step 4

Use the grid to draw Mickey.

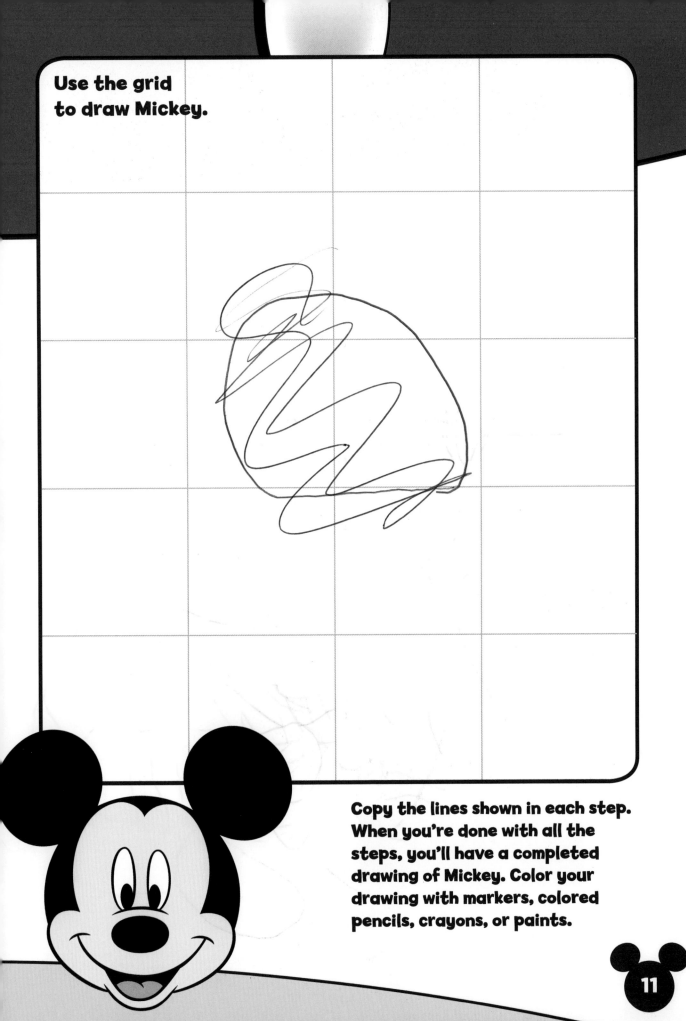

Copy the lines shown in each step. When you're done with all the steps, you'll have a completed drawing of Mickey. Color your drawing with markers, colored pencils, crayons, or paints.

Follow along, first drawing basic shapes with light pencil lines. Copy the new lines shown in each step, eventually darkening the lines you want to keep and erasing the rest. Finally add color to your drawing with colored pencils, markers, paints, or crayons.

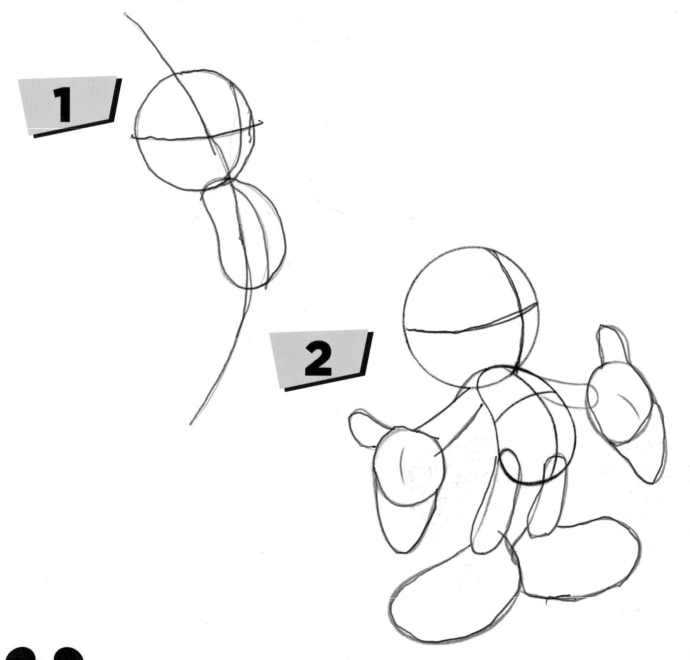

1

2

3

5

6

Practice drawing
Mickey here.

MINNIE MOUSE

Minnie is a free-spirited, active mouse with intelligence and endless interests. She plunges herself into all kinds of adventures, especially the fun kind! Minnie has a special bond with animals, nature, and, of course, her boyfriend, Mickey, and the rest of her friends!

Use the tracing paper to draw Minnie.

Step 1

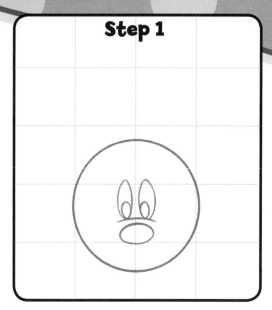

Step 2

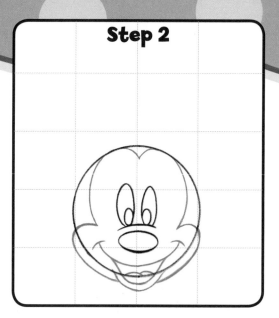

Step 3

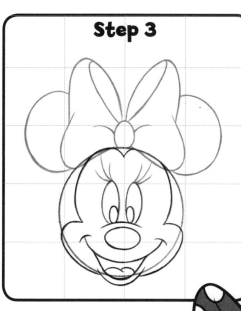

Step 4

Use the grid to draw Minnie.

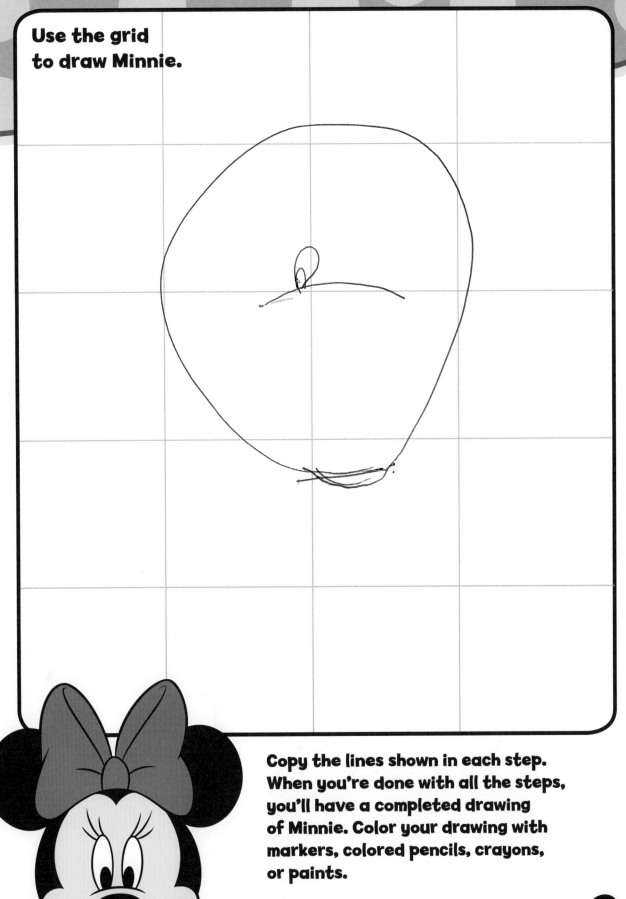

Copy the lines shown in each step. When you're done with all the steps, you'll have a completed drawing of Minnie. Color your drawing with markers, colored pencils, crayons, or paints.

21

Follow along, first drawing basic shapes with light pencil lines. Copy the new lines shown in each step, eventually darkening the lines you want to keep and erasing the rest. Finally add color to your drawing with colored pencils, markers, paints, or crayons.

1

2

3

4

6

PLUTO

Pluto is full grown but has the spirit of a puppy. He is friendly, happy, and always ready to play, but he can become a tough guard dog when necessary. He is a loyal companion, always there for Mickey, who also happens to be his owner.

Use the tracing paper to draw Pluto.

Step 1

Step 2

Step 3

Step 4

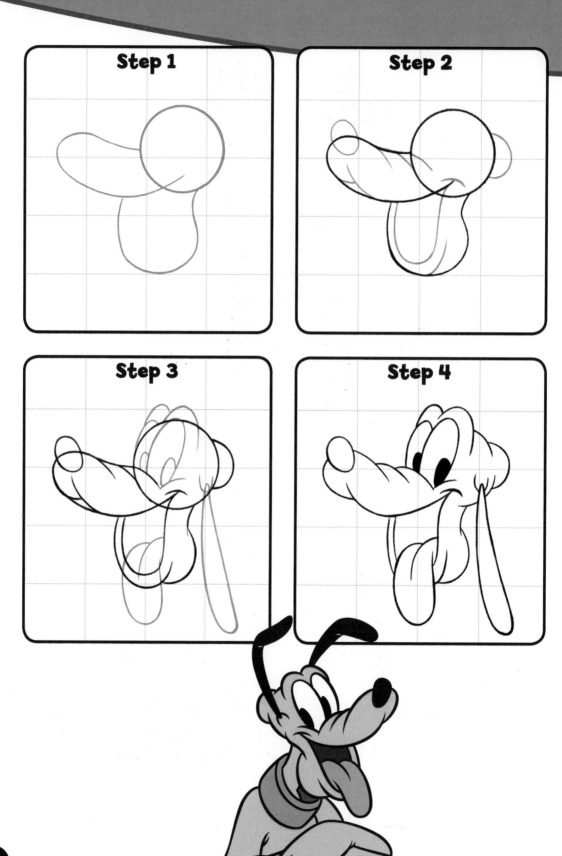

Use the grid to draw Pluto.

Copy the lines shown in each step. When you're done with all the steps, you'll have a completed drawing of Pluto. Color your drawing with markers, colored pencils, crayons, or paints.

Follow along, copying the
new lines shown in each
step. Darken the lines you
want to keep and erase
the rest, and then color
your drawing!

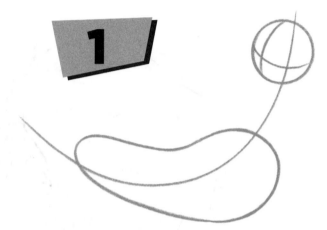

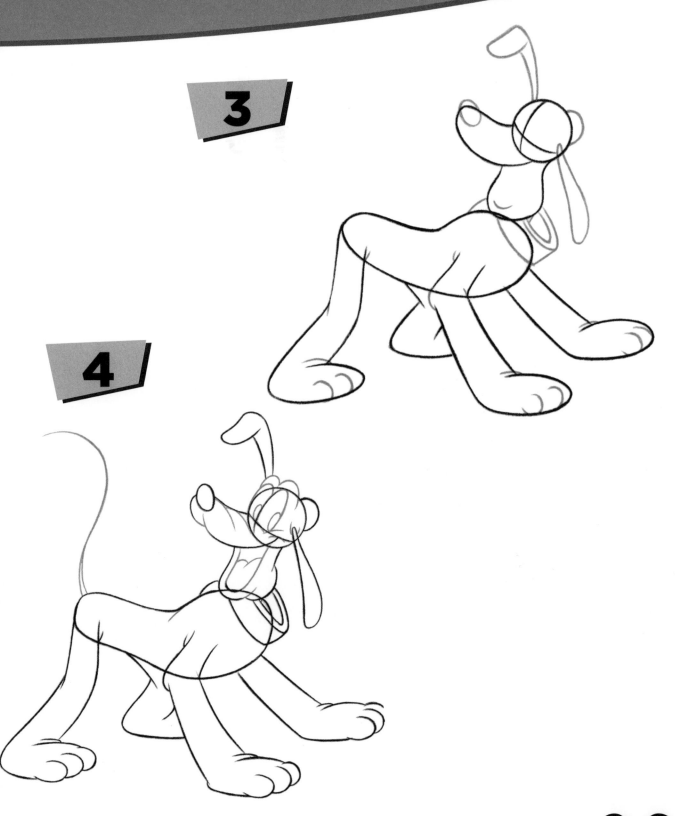

3

4

5

6

GOOFY

Goofy has a sensitive soul and becomes very attached to things—such as his now-ancient car—and he would rather store everything in his chaotic attic rather than throw it away. There's nothing Goofy wouldn't do for his friends—especially his best friend, Mickey.

Use the tracing paper to draw Goofy.

Step 1

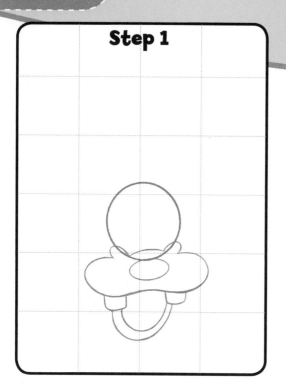

Step 2

Step 3

Step 4

Copy the lines shown in each step. When you're done with all the steps, you'll have a completed drawing of Goofy. Color your drawing with markers, colored pencils, crayons, or paints.

Use the grid to draw Goofy.

Follow along, copying the new lines shown in each step. Darken the lines you want to keep and erase the rest, and then color your drawing!

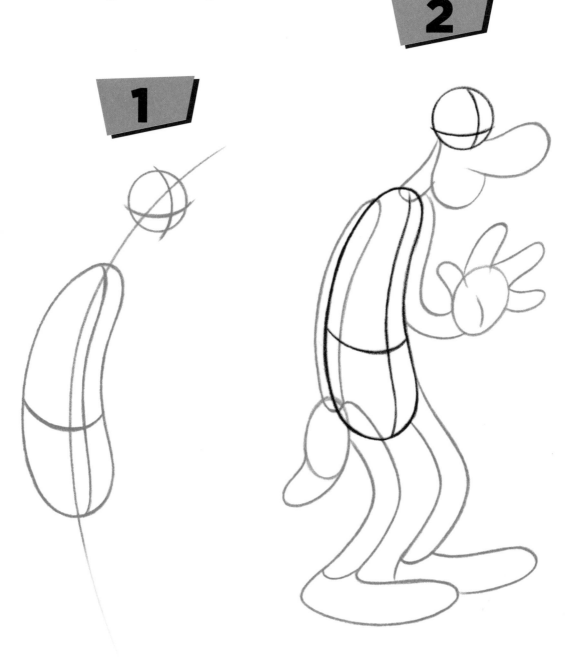

1

2

3

4

5

6

Practice drawing Goofy here.

$5 + 5 = \boxed{10}$

$10 + 10 = \boxed{20}$

DONALD DUCK

Donald Duck has quite a temper, but despite his ways, it's hard not to like him. He goes on all sorts of adventures, certain that he'll be successful in whatever he tries. But because he always takes the quickest and easiest route, he ends up on the path to total disaster!

Use the tracing paper to draw Donald.

Follow along, first drawing basic shapes with light pencil lines. Copy the new lines shown in each step, eventually darkening the lines you want to keep and erasing the rest. Finally add color to your drawing with colored pencils, markers, paints, or crayons.

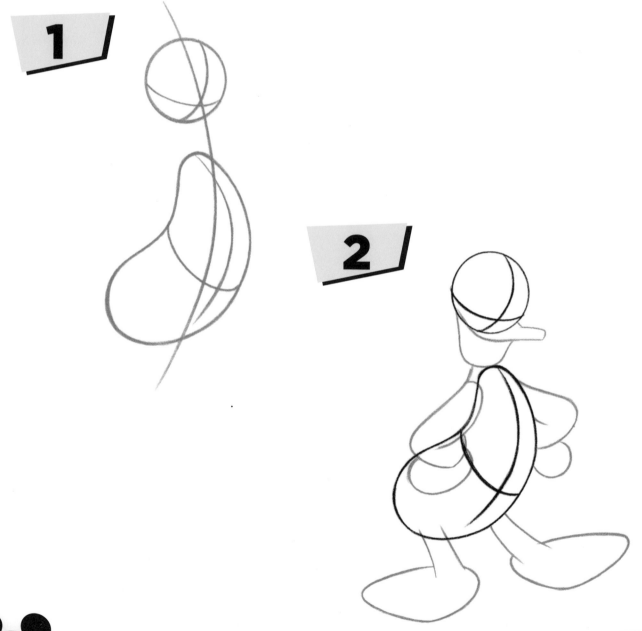

3

4

5

6

02 to 240

つ to 02 x 23

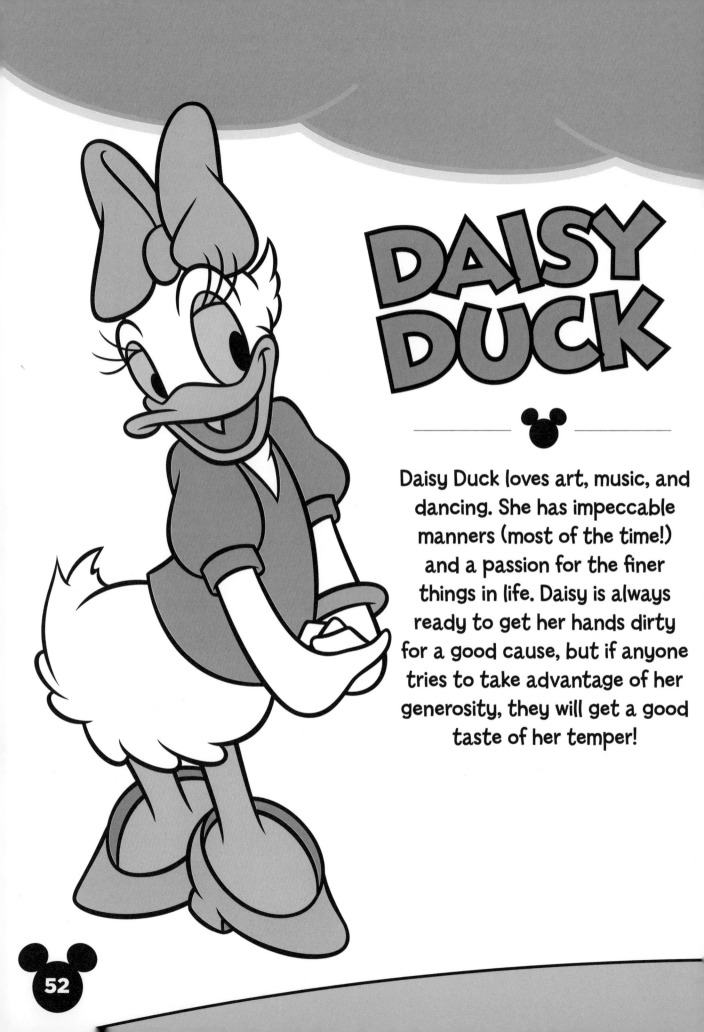

DAISY DUCK

Daisy Duck loves art, music, and dancing. She has impeccable manners (most of the time!) and a passion for the finer things in life. Daisy is always ready to get her hands dirty for a good cause, but if anyone tries to take advantage of her generosity, they will get a good taste of her temper!

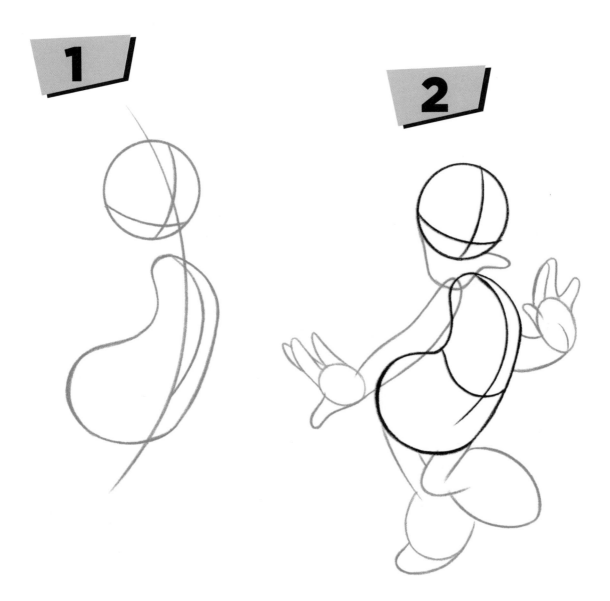

Follow along, copying the new lines shown in each
step. Darken the lines you want to keep and
erase the rest, and then color your drawing!

1

2

3

4

5

6

Practice drawing
Daisy here.

HUEY, DEWEY & LOUIE

Triplets Huey, Dewey & Louie are intelligent practical jokers who sometimes make life difficult for their Uncle Donald. They act and look very similar, and the only way to tell them apart visually is by the color of their caps: red for Huey, blue for Dewey, and green for Louie.

Just like you've done before, follow the steps to draw Huey, Dewey & Louie. Then add color!

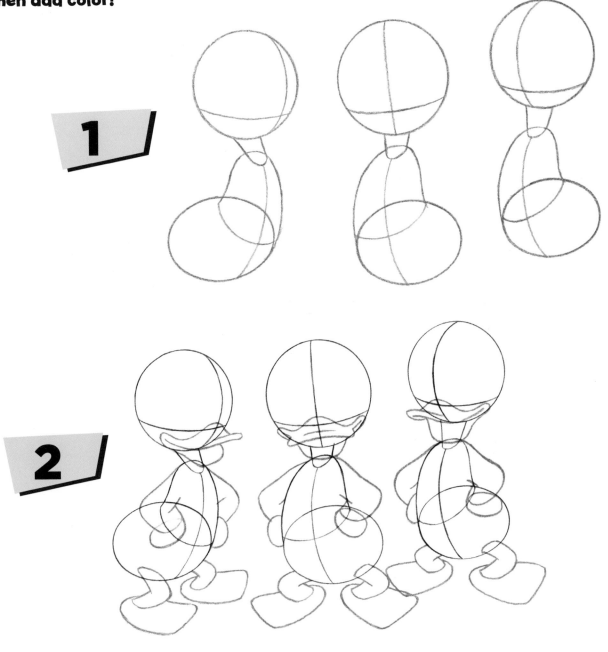

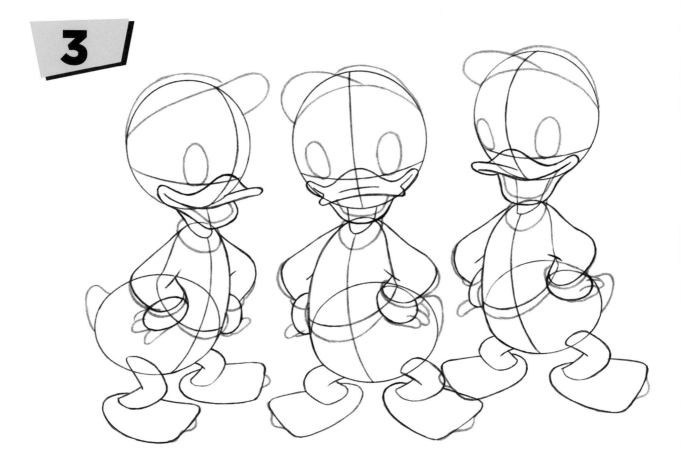

4

5

Don't miss these other books by Walter Foster Jr.!

Learn to Draw Disney
Classic Animated Movies
Draw characters from *Alice in Wonderland,*
The Jungle Book, Fantasia, 101 Dalmatians,
Peter Pan, The Fox and the Hound, Bambi,
Pinocchio, Lady and the Tramp, The
Aristocats, and *Dumbo.*
ISBN: 978-1-63322-135-2

Learn to Draw
Disney Princesses
Learn to draw beautiful portraits of all
your favorite Disney Princesses, including
Snow White, Cinderella, Ariel, Belle,
Mulan, and more!
ISBN: 978-1-63322-662-3

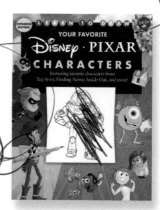

Learn to Draw Your Favorite
Disney•Pixar Characters
You can draw characters from *Toy Story,*
Monsters Inc., Finding Nemo, The Incredibles,
Cars, Up, Inside Out, Coco, and more.
ISBN: 978-1-63322-677-7

Visit QuartoKnows.com for more Learn to Draw Disney books.